Fire

by Henry Pluckrose

Gareth Stevens Publishing
A WORLD ALMANAC EDUCATION GROUP COMPANY

Please visit our web site at: www.garethstevens.com
For a free color catalog describing Gareth Stevens' list of high-quality books
and multimedia programs, call 1-800-542-2595 (USA) or 1-800-461-9120 (Canada).
Gareth Stevens Publishing's Fax: (414) 332-3567.

Library of Congress Cataloging-in-Publication Data

Pluckrose, Henry Arthur.
    Fire / by Henry Pluckrose. — North American ed.
      p. cm. — (Let's explore)
    Includes bibliographical references and index.
    ISBN 0-8368-2961-1 (lib. bdg.)
    1. Fire—Juvenile literature. 2. Combustion—Juvenile literature.
  [1. Fire. 2. Combustion.] I. Title.
  TP265.P55   2001
  621.402'3—dc21   2001031114

This North American edition first published in 2001 by
Gareth Stevens Publishing
A World Almanac Education Group Company
330 West Olive Street, Suite 100
Milwaukee, WI 53212 USA

This U.S. edition © 2001 by Gareth Stevens, Inc. Original edition © 2000 by Franklin Watts.
First published in 2000 by Franklin Watts, 96 Leonard Street, London, EC2A 4XD, United
Kingdom. Additional end matter © 2001 by Gareth Stevens, Inc.

Series editor: Louise John
Series designer: Jason Anscomb
Gareth Stevens editor: Monica Rausch
Gareth Stevens designer: Katherine A. Kroll

Picture credits: Images Colour Library pp. 4, 23, 31; Impact pp. 16, 17 (Jeremy Nicholl);
Tony Stone Images p. 20 and title page (David Austen); Still Pictures pp. 9 (Mark Edwards),
27 (Reinhard Janke); Oxford Scientific Films p. 24 (David Cayless); Planet Earth Pictures p. 6
(Bryan and Cherry Alexander); Robert Harding pp. 10 (Yoav Levy/Phototake NYC), 15
(Richard Ashworth), 28 (N. Francis); Firepix International p. 19 (Tony Myers); Ray Moller
Photography p. 12.

Printed in the United States of America

1 2 3 4 5 6 7 8 9 05 04 03 02 01

Contents

The Sun may look like a ball of fire, but it is actually not fire at all. The Sun is made of very hot gases. These gases give off heat and light.

Fire gives off heat and light — just like the Sun.

In the past, people needed fire to keep warm, to cook food, and to see in the dark.

We often use matches to start a fire. A match is a thin piece of cardboard or wood with a special mixture of chemicals on its tip. We must be very careful when we use matches. The chemicals burst into flame when the match is rubbed against a rough surface.

A fire needs fuel to burn. The fuel for the fire in this fireplace is wood.

Fire also needs a gas called oxygen. Oxygen is in the air around us. Without oxygen, a fire will die.

Fire is dangerous!
The heat from a
fire can burn you.
Smoke from a fire
can make it hard
for you to breathe.

Firefighters wear special clothes to protect themselves from fires. Why do you think this firefighter is wearing a mask?

Sometimes firefighters use foam to stop a fire. The foam covers the burning material. It prevents oxygen in the air from reaching the fire, so the fire dies.

Forest fires can spread quickly, especially when the wind blows. Sometimes firefighters drop water from airplanes to put out forest fires or to keep them from spreading.

Although fire is dangerous, if we are careful, we can use the power of fire. We can use fire to cook our food.

Some people use fire at work. A blacksmith uses fire to heat a piece of iron. When the iron is very hot, it becomes soft. The blacksmith can bend and shape the soft iron to make many different objects. What is this blacksmith making?

A glassmaker builds a fire in a large oven, or furnace, to heat sand until it melts into a hot liquid. The glassmaker blows air into the liquid to make different shapes. When the liquid cools, it becomes glass.

Sometimes we light big fires outdoors to celebrate special events. These fires are called bonfires.

We also celebrate special events with fireworks. Fireworks are filled with gunpowder. Gunpowder explodes and makes a loud noise when it is lit by fire. Fireworks, like fire, are dangerous. We must always be careful to keep the power of fire under control.

Index

More Books to Read

All Aboard Fire Trucks. All Aboard (series).
   Teddy Slater (Price Stern Sloan)

A Day with Firefighters. Hard Work (series).
   Jan Kottke (Children's Press)

Fire. Let's Find Out (series). Kitty Benedict and
   Andrienne Soutter-Perrot (Creative Education)